Tapping for Zapping

GoTapping! Nelly Learns The Emotional Freedom Technique (EFT) for Kids

Written by Renee Jain

Illustrated by Shahab Shamshirsaz

Author: Renee Jain
Illustrator: Shahab Shamshirsaz
Layout Designer: Nikki Abramowitz

ISBN: 1516906365
ISBN-13: 978-1-5169-0636-9

If you change the way you look at things,
the things you look at change.

-Wayne Dyer

"Nelly, let's go! The bus is almost here!"

"Dad, can you drive me to school today?" Nelly asked. "Pleeeeeeeease?"

"I can't today, honey," he said, as he grabbed his briefcase. "Let's go. I'll walk you to the bus stop."

Nelly furrowed her brow. She hated the bus and wished her Dad could just drop her off on his way to work.

"Please, Dad. Please can you drive me? It'll only take you an extra minute," Nelly begged.

"Not today, honey. I have an early meeting." Then he crouched down next to her, rubbed her back, and whispered, "Come on, Nell, we've been through this. You'll be fine. I promise. Okay?"

"Fine," Nelly pouted. But she didn't want to upset her Dad, so she perked up and continued, "You're right, Daddy, I'll be fine." Then she walked out the door, feeling as nervous as ever.

As Nelly approached the bus stop, she tried to make out the faces of the kids waiting, but she couldn't focus. Thoughts were racing through her head:

Will anyone talk to me?

Should I say hello first?

What if no one wants to sit with me... again?

Nelly rested her hand on her tummy, hoping it would settle down. Then, she quickly moved it up to her heart to keep it from leaping out of her chest. To say she was nervous was a serious understatement. By the time she reached the bus stop, beads of sweat were steadily trickling down her forehead.

She stole a few glances at the other kids. A couple of girls were whispering and giggling with each other. A boy with red hair was digging into his lunch box. No one looked at Nelly, so she just fiddled with her hands as if they were the most interesting things in the entire universe.

Until, that is, she saw a blue flash out of the corner of her eye. *What was that?*

Wait, was that kid wearing a blue costume? No, it wasn't a costume, it was her *skin*! Oh, of course, it was Neutrino, the lanky blue alien with pointy ears and humongous green eyes who was visiting Nelly's town of Fliderdale. Neutrino arrived a couple of months ago; she said she was there to "spread more happiness to humanoids"... whatever that meant.

Neutrino walked over while twisting and turning her body in the strangest way—it looked painful. Nelly thought it was probably a type of alien greeting.

"Hi, Neutrino. Are you OK?" Nelly asked.

"Hello youthling Nelly, forgive me. I just left a moontop party where everyone was doing the ZootyBooty dance. I, too, was zooting out when I felt the stress level in Fliderdale spike. I traced it back to this spot—what's going on, youthling? What bothers you?"

Nelly looked over at the other kids. She was silent.

"I see. You worry what the other youthlings will think. Just a momentino." Neutrino snapped her fingers, and just like that, the kids were motionless.

In fact, everything was perfectly still—*she had frozen the entire town.*

"Speak freely, youthling," said Neutrino. "What disturbs your well-being?"

Nelly peeled her eyes away from her immobile classmates and explained, "I hate taking the bus."

"You mean the big, yellow motorized carriage that delivers you to school? It seems perfectly harmless."

"Well, it... it smells."

"Smells?"

"Yes, like feet." Nelly was a terrible liar.

Neutrino yanked off her space boots, pushed her right foot directly up to her nose, and took a big sniff.

"Youthling, I would love to ride in a motorized carriage that smells like lavendria bush," she smiled. "I infuse my energy baths with this plant."

Nelly cracked a smile. Neutrino was quirky, even for an alien.

Neutrino was silent for a moment and gazed at Nelly until she felt compelled to say more.

"The truth is, I get really worried when I have to take the bus. This year I'm going to a different school than most of my friends. My dad told me to just be friendly, so last week I asked a girl if I could sit next to her, and she just turned away from me. It was so embarrassing. On top of it, the bus driver started screaming at me."

"What did she scream?" asked Neutrino.

Nelly took a deep breath and mimicked in a loud, squeaky voice, ***"Hey, kid, FIND A SEAT ALREADY!"***

Nelly began to tear up.

"Oh youthling, please do not leak water from your eyes," Neutrino said. "I think I can help you feel less nervous. You just need a quick reboot."

"I'm not a computer, Neutrino. I can't reboot."

"Sure you can. On Eudaimonia, we reboot our well-being all the time!"

Nelly looked totally confused. Neutrino tried to explain, "You see, youthling, your chi is muddled up. All you need to do is GoTapping! and you'll feel much better. Get it?"

Nelly didn't understand a word of what Neutrino was saying. Humans don't reboot or "go tapping." And did she say something about cheese? Nelly decided Neutrino wasn't going to be much help.

"Hey, um, I have to get to school. Maybe you could just please unfreeze everything and let me go?"

"Yes, I will do that after we GoTapping! to release your chi!" Neutrino repeated.

Wow, Nelly thought, *she's not giving up.* "Neutrino, I'm trying to explain to you that people on Earth don't go tapping or reboot, and we aren't made of cheese! I thought you wanted to help me feel less nervous. Can you please just let me go to school so I'm not late?"

"Fliderdale is frozen, youthling, you will not be late. Right now, you must meet someone." Neutrino snapped her fingers.

"But..." before Nelly could finish, they were flying. "Whoa, where are we going? Wait, is that the Great Wall of China?" Nelly recognized it from her history book. Neutrino smiled, and before Nelly knew it, they landed.

"We're at a bus stop again, but where are we?" Nelly wondered out loud.

"We are at a bus stop in Beijing, youthling."

Neutrino started walking toward a boy about Nelly's age. He didn't seem to see them because he was busy doing something very strange—poking himself under his eye and mumbling something. Nelly was sure he said, "I'm totally nervous." Then he started poking himself under his nose and mumbling it again. He finally noticed Neutrino.

"Neutrino, how are you?"

"Hello, youthling Lok!"

They did a fist bump, and then started doing the ZootyBooty dance. Nelly guessed they knew each other well.

"Lok, please meet youthling Nelly," Neutrino said to the boy. "Nelly is feeling very worried about going on a yellow motorized carriage to school. I thought you might be able to help."

"Hey, Nelly. So the school bus makes you nervous, huh?"

"Sometimes, I guess. Well, most of the time, actually," Nelly confessed. "By the way, what were you doing to your face when we got here?"

"Oh, you saw me," Lok smiled. "I think that's what Neutrino wants me to tell you about. See, I get nervous too... not about getting on the bus, but before I play sports—especially baseball. I love baseball, but I used to get so nervous before games that sometimes I would just stay at home and tell my coach I was sick.

"One day, my grandfather saw that I was faking being sick, and I had to tell him what was going on. Grandfather said he was going to teach me about chi so I could feel less nervous before games."

"There's that word again... did you say 'cheese'?"

"Ha ha, I guess it sounds like that. Chi. It's pronounced chee. It means energy and it travels around our bodies."

"Lok, it's really nice that you want to teach me about chi and stuff, but I don't think we have that where I come from."

Neutrino cackled, "Hee hoo. Ha ho. Hee hum. Oh, you made a funny, youthling, the universe is made of energy... It's everywhere, including inside of you. While Lok is calling it *chi*, in Indian cultures they call it *prana*, in ancient Greece it was called *pneuma*, and Hawaiian culture refers to it as *mana*. I could go on youthling. My favorite term comes from Western culture... have you heard of *The Force*?"

"Neutrino, that's from Star Wars... that's a movie, not reality," Nelly explained.

"So much to learn you have, youthling."

Nelly shook her head and said, "Okay, I get it. There's energy everywhere, including inside the body, and different cultures call it different names. What I don't really understand is how that can help me feel less nervous when I'm getting on the bus."

Lok continued, "Grandfather taught me that chi travels through the body along these paths, kind of like super highways. When your chi is flowing normally, you feel great. But sometimes there's a traffic jam, and the chi gets stuck. And when that happens, it can make you feel bad or sad or nervous or a combination of things."

"What makes chi get stuck?" Nelly asked.

"I asked Grandpa the same thing! He said if we think worried *thoughts* or have nervous *feelings*, chi can get stuck. Hey, Neutrino, can you show Nelly an image?"

Snap!

Energy Superhighways Inside the Body

"Whoa. That looks really complicated, like something you'd learn in science class," Nelly said.

"I know! But actually it's pretty simple. You just have to get the chi moving again."

"But didn't you say chi or this energy is moving *inside* the body? How can we fix it if it's on the inside?"

"I haven't told you the best part yet. There are special points called *meridian points* on our skin that can tap into your chi."

"So you were tapping on those points earlier? But it looks like from that image there are bajillions of... what did you call them? Meridian points?"

"There are! Sometimes it takes a lifetime to learn about how to work with meridian points and chi—Grandpa has been studying it since he was a kid. But get this, Neutrino came along and taught me a way to work with my chi that's really simple. She took me on a trip to your part of the world, and I learned a method called *tapping*."

"You learned this from my part of the world?" asked Nelly.

Neutrino jumped in, "That's right, Nelly, humanoid scientists all over the world have started to work to make energy flow better in the body. Tapping is just one way to do this."

"I think I'm starting to get it now. Tapping on certain places on my body will make my chi or energy flow better, and then I won't be as nervous. But what if I can't help the thoughts going through my head? What if I can't help the feelings I feel when I'm really nervous, like when my stomach is doing flip-flops? My dad tells me to think positive, but I just can't help what I'm feeling and thinking, you know?"

Neutrino responded, "Youthling, once you start tapping the way Lok will show you, your chi will flow better and you will naturally have fewer upsetting thoughts and feelings. You just have to try it."

Lok jumped in, "And it's really simple to learn! See, there are nine tapping points we use. Neutrino, can you hook us up with another image please?"

Snap!

Tapping Points

1. Karate Chop
2. Inner Eyebrow
3. Side of Eye
4. Under the Eye
5. Under the Nose
6. Chin
7. Collarbone
8. Under Armpit
9. Top of the Head

1. **Karate Chop -** the outside edge of your hand, below your little finger

2. **Inner Eyebrow -** on the end of either eyebrow, near the bridge of your nose

3. **Side of Eye -** the outside of either eye, on the bone

4. **Under the Eye -** about an inch below either eye, on the bone

5. **Under the Nose -** above your upper lip

6. **Chin -** below your lower lip, where your chin starts

7. **Collarbone -** the inside end of either collarbone, below your throat

8. **Under Armpit -** about four inches down, on the side of your rib cage

9. **Top of the Head -** in line with your ears on the top of your head

"Cool!" Lok and Nelly said together.

"We're going to tap on each point with two fingers in the order you see on the image," explained Lok. He held out two of his fingers like he was pointing and began tapping the side of his hand or the "Karate Chop" area to demonstrate.

"Each time you tap on a different part, you're going to say some words out loud."

"What words do I say? How do I start?" Nelly asked.

Neutrino responded, "First take a couple deep breaths, and then start with an 'even though' statement. Like this:

"Even though _____, I still deeply love and accept myself."

In the blank, put what you are worried about. For example,

"Even though, I am very worried about taking the bus, I still deeply love and accept myself."

Nelly started laughing. "Did you say, 'I deeply love and accept myself?' That's a little corny, Neutrino."

"Ha ha!" Lok laughed. "Here's the one I just used."

"Even though I think I'm going to strike out when I get to bat and it makes me feel totally nervous, I'm still an awesome kid."

"I like that, Lok," Nelly said, smiling.

Lok continued, "I start tapping and say my 'even though' statement three times, and then I tap everywhere else using reminder words."

"How many times do you tap and which hand do I use?" Nelly asked. "And what exactly are reminder words?"

"Tap each point about five to seven times and you can use either hand—it doesn't matter. Bend your fingers so your hand is relaxed. You know what, how about I just show you? It'll be easier."

Lok took a few deep breaths in and out and then started tapping.

1. He tapped on the Karate chop area:
"Even though I think I'm going to strike out when I get to bat and it makes me feel totally nervous, I'm still an awesome kid." He repeated this three times, while continuing to tap the karate chop area.

2. He tapped his inner eyebrow: *"I'm totally nervous."*

3. He tapped the side of his eye: *"I'm totally nervous."*

4. He tapped under his eye: *"I'm totally nervous."*

5. He tapped under his nose: *"I'm totally nervous."*

6. He tapped his chin: *"I'm totally nervous."*

7. He tapped his collarbone: *"Yup, I'm totally nervous."*

8. He tapped under his armpit: *"I'm totally nervous."*

9. Finally, he tapped the top of his head:
"I'm totally nervous."

"You wanna try it?" Lok gently asked Nelly.

Nelly decided to give it a chance, but right before she started, she worried out loud, "Wait, what if I don't get it right? What if I don't tap each point the right amount of times or say the right words?"

Neutrino said gently, "Youthling, there is no right or wrong. Do not concern yourself with counting or the precise wording. Let's begin like this: Tell us a little bit about how you feel when you have to go on the motorized carriage."

Nelly sighed and then explained, "Every time I think about walking to the bus stop, it feels like there are butterflies flying all around in my stomach. I keep thinking everyone is going to stare and giggle because I don't have anyone to sit with. Then last week after the bus driver yelled at me, I felt ten times worse. I'm really worried about getting on the bus and being laughed at and yelled at again."

"Thank you for sharing, youthling," Neutrino comforted. "It is good to express your worry. Want to GoTapping! on that worry now? Start with a few deep breaths."

Nelly took a few deep breaths and then stuck out her two fingers and started tapping.

1. She tapped her karate chop area and repeated three times: *"Even though I'm super worried about getting on the bus and being laughed at and yelled at, I'm still an awesome kid."*

2. She tapped at her inner eyebrow: *"I'm super worried."*

3. She tapped her outer eye: *"Super worried."*

4. She tapped under her eye: *"Super duper worried."*

5. She tapped under her nose: *"I'm super worried."*

6. She tapped her chin: *"I'm really worried."*

7. She tapped her collarbone: *"I'm super worried."*

8. She tapped under her armpit: *"Super worried!"*

9. Finally, Nelly tapped on the top of her head: *"I'm worried."*

Nelly took a deep breath when she was done.

Lok anxiously asked, "Soooo... how do you feel?"

Nelly thought about it. She said, "I actually feel a little better."

"Woohoo! You feel a little better! It takes some practice, but the amazing thing is that you can do it anywhere!" Lok exclaimed.

"Fantastalicious to the ultra-astronomical power!" Neutrino said, clapping.

Nelly and Lok laughed.

Neutrino grabbed Nelly's hand and said, "Come along, time to get you back to your yellow carriage."

Nelly and Lok gave each other a high five and a fist bump. Lok started to do the ZootyBooty dance, and Nelly tried her best to twist and turn her body.

"Alrighty then, Nelly, great to meet you," Lok said.

Snap!

And with that, Neutrino and Nelly flew home. In no time, they were back at Nelly's bus stop.

"Ready?" Neutrino asked.

"Ready," Nelly replied. Neutrino snapped again, and everything went back to normal. The leaves moved in the wind, the little girls told their secrets, and the boy with the red hair finished his snack. Then the bus pulled up.

Nelly took a deep breath and climbed up the stairs slowly, one step at a time. She felt confident as she walked down the aisle and even made eye contact with a girl named Roberta Morris from her math class. Roberta gave her a smile and slid over on her seat a bit, making it clear she wanted Nelly to join her. Nelly and Roberta chatted the entire ride to school.

That night, Nelly lay awake in bed. She was happy she got through the day, but then grew concerned about having to do it all over again tomorrow. She rolled over in bed and looked out the window at the stars.

"They are magicatastical, aren't they?" asked Neutrino, as she floated in through Nelly's window.

"Hey, Neutrino," Nelly said and sat up in bed.

"There is a small ripple in your well-being again, youthling. Did you not have a good day today?"

"I did," said Nelly, "But what if I'm worried again tomorrow?"

"Youthling, let me see if I understand, you are *worried* about being *worried?*"

"Haha, I guess you're right, Neutrino... I am worried about being worried."

"That is no problem. You can GoTapping! any time, and the more you tap, the less you will worry. Would you like to try it again right now?"

Nelly nodded and took a few deep breaths.

1. She tapped her karate chop area and repeated three times: *"Even though I'm worried about feeling worried again, I still deeply love and accept myself."* Neutrino smiled.

2. She tapped her inner eyebrow: *"Worried about worry."*

3. She tapped her outer eye: *"Worried about worry."*

4. She tapped under her eye: *"Worried about worry."*

5. She tapped under her nose: *"Worried about worry."*

6. She tapped under her chin: *"Worried about worry."*

7. She tapped at her collarbone: *"Worried about worry."*

8. She tapped under her armpit: *"Worried about worry."*

9. She tapped the top of her head: *"Worried about worry."*

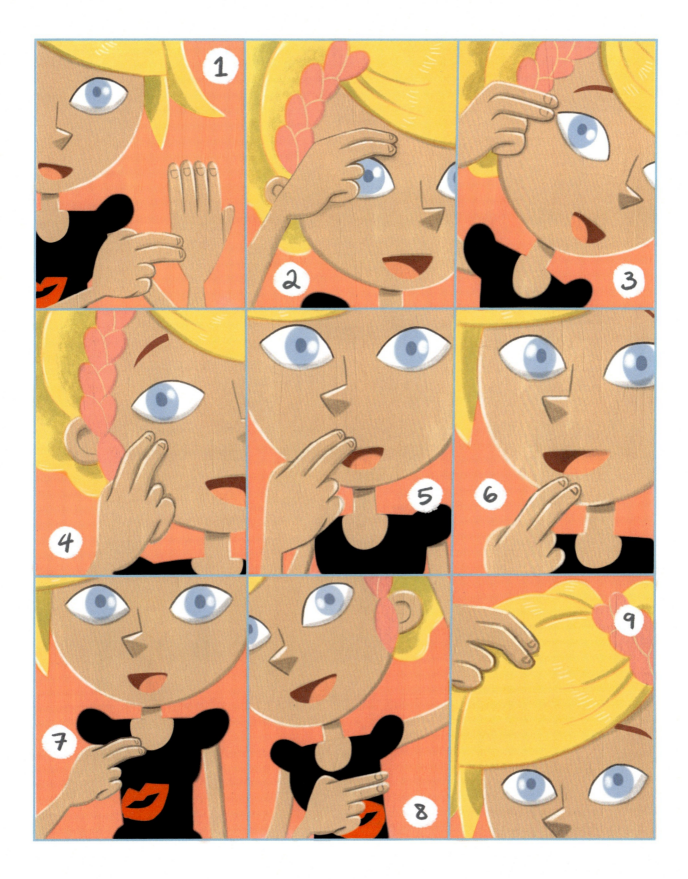

Nelly took a deep breath in and then exhaled out slowly when she was done. She felt peaceful. She looked at the alien who was sitting on her bed and gave her a smile of true gratitude. "Thank you, Neutrino."

"You are most welcome, youthling. Fare thee well," Neutrino replied softly and then flew off into the night.

Get your GoTapping! Bonuses

Neutrino would love to send you a gift! Get early access to the animated videos and webinars that go along with this book. If you'd like early access to these resources and lots of cool bonus stuff, all you have to do is visit:

www.gozen.com/gotapping

GoTapping! 5-Step Bonus Worksheet

Step 1. What situation is causing you to feel worried, stressed, or anxious?

_____

_____

_____

_____

_____

Step 2. Circle how worried you are from 1-10 on the well-being scale below:

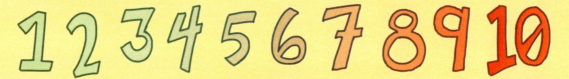

Relaxed	Nervous	Super Worried
Happy	Upset	Panicked!
Peaceful	Worried	

Step 3. Create an 'even though' statement using one of the options from below. Insert what you are worrying about in the blank space. Next, write down a few reminder words that remind you of the situation you're worrying about.

Even though _____

_____, I still deeply love and accept myself.

    OR

Even though _____

_____, I'm still an awesome kid.

    OR

Even though _____

_____, I _____.

Reminder words (choose a few words as a reminder of the

worry): _____

Step 4. GoTapping! You can tap 5-7 times on each point, but don't worry about counting or being precise... do what feels comfortable. Use the same pressure you would use strumming your fingers on a table.

Take a few deep breaths and begin:

1. **Karate Chop:** 'even though' statement three times
2. **Inner Eyebrow:** reminder words
3. **Side of Eye:** reminder words
4. **Under the Eye:** reminder words
5. **Under the Nose:** reminder words
6. **Chin:** reminder words
7. **Collarbone:** reminder words
8. **Under Armpit:** reminder words
9. **Top of the head:** reminder words

Step 5. Take a deep breath when you're done. Circle how you feel on the well-being scale again. Keep tapping until you reduce your worry down. Be kind and gentle with yourself. Tapping takes a little practice. :)

1 2 3 4 5 6 7 8 9 10

Relaxed
Happy
Peaceful

Nervous
Upset
Worried

Super Worried
Panicked!

The Science

"Tapping is the most impressive intervention I've encountered in 25 years of work."

-Rick Leskowitz, Harvard Medical School psychiatrist, director of the Integrative Medicine Project at Spaulding Rehabilitation Hospital

For those parents, educators, and children who like to get into the nitty gritty science of what is interchangeably called Energy Psychology, The Emotional Freedom Technique, or tapping, here are some research studies as well as some food for thought.

How does tapping work?

Tapping melds Western clinical methods (exposure therapy and cognitive restructuring) with Eastern healing practices of acupressure (akin to acupuncture or stimulation of targeted pressure points without needles). You will see from the citations below there are many randomized controlled trials revealing the powerful effects of tapping, but the mechanism by which it works is still being explored.

A good working hypothesis has been proposed by David Feinstien, Ph.D., co-author of *Energy Medicine for Women* and a clinical psychologist who has served on the faculties of The Johns Hopkins University School of Medicine, Antioch College, & the California School of Professional Psychology. Feinstein says tapping works as "bringing to mind an emotional trigger, problematic scene, or unresolved traumatic memory activates the amygdala, arousing a threat response. Stimulating selected acupoints, according to the Harvard studies, simultaneously sends deactivating signals to the amygdala."

In other words, when you expose yourself to a negative belief or traumatic memory (exposure therapy) and then practice self-acceptance (cognitive restructuring) while simultaneously tapping on acupressure points, a calming signal is sent to the brain. In the end, your brain creates new positive associations with the memory that no longer triggers the stress or anxiety response.

More on the research:

Tapping has been demonstrated to be so effective, it is being used to treat several conditions including PTSD, depression, and anxiety. Here is a sample of research studies:

Baker, A. H., & Siegel, M. A. (2010). Emotional Freedom Techniques (EFT) reduces intense fears: A partial replication and extension of Wells et al. Energy Psychology: Theory, Research, & Treatment, 2(2), p 13-30.

Boath, E., Carryer, A., & Stewart, A. (2013). Is Emotional Freedom Techniques (EFT) Generalizable? Comparing Effects in Sport Science Students Versus Complementary Therapy Students. *EPJ Energy Psychology Journal.*

Bougea, A., Spandideas, N., Alexopoulos, E., Thomaides, T., Chrousos, G., & Darviri, C. (n.d.). Effect of the Emotional Freedom Technique on Perceived Stress, Quality of Life, and Cortisol Salivary Levels in Tension-Type Headache Sufferers: A Randomized Controlled Trial. *EXPLORE: The Journal of Science and Healing*, 91-99.

Burk, L. (2010). Single session EFT (Emotional Freedom Techniques) for stress-related symptoms after motor vehicle accidents. Energy Psychology: Theory, Research, & Treatment, (2010), 2(1), 65-72.

Church, D. (n.d.). Reductions in Pain, Depression, and Anxiety Symptoms After PTSD Remediation in Veterans. *EXPLORE: The Journal of Science and Healing*, 162-169.

Church, D. (2010). The Effect of EFT (Emotional Freedom Techniques) on Athletic Performance: A Randomized Controlled Blind Trial. *The Open Sports Sciences Journal TOSSJ*, 94-99.

Church, D., Piña, O., Reategui, C., & Brooks, A. (2011). Single session reduction of the intensity of traumatic memories in abused adolescents after EFT: A randomized controlled pilot study. *Traumatology.* doi:10.1177/1534765611426788

Feinstein, D. (n.d.). Acupoint stimulation in treating psychological disorders: Evidence of efficacy. *Review of General Psychology,* 364-380.

Jain, S., & Rubino, A. (2012). The Effectiveness of Emotional Freedom Techniques for Optimal Test Performance. *EPJ Energy Psychology Journal.*

Jones, S., Thornton, J., & Andrews, H. (2011). Efficacy of Emotional Freedom Techniques (EFT) in Reducing Public Speaking Anxiety: A Randomized Controlled Trial. *EPJ Energy Psychology Journal.*

Palmer-Hoffman, J., & Brooks, A. (2011). Psychological Symptom Change after Group Application of Emotional Freedom Techniques (EFT). *EPJ Energy Psychology Journal.*

Sezgin, N., & Ozcan, B. (2009). The Effect of Progressive Muscular Relaxation and Emotional Freedom Techniques on Test Anxiety in High School Students: A Randomized Controlled Trial. *EPJ Energy Psychology Journal,* 23-29.

About the Author: Chief Storyteller

I'm Renee Jain, the founder and Chief Storyteller at GoZen! Growing up, I was always worried. At five years old I begged my parents to let me sleep with my brother's yellow plastic bat because I was so worried that when I went to sleep, a robber would break in. I know all too well what it's like to live with anxiety as a child.

As I grew up, I continued to struggle until one day I had a panic attack in my office. As I lay gasping for breath, I decided enough was enough. I wasn't going to let anxiety control my life any longer. I spent several years investing time in self-education, talk therapy and then a master's in psychology. Through both formal education and personal experience, one very clear truth emerged: Resilience is a skill.

While some of us are born more resilient, others simply need to master this ability with practice (and, yes, it can be practiced)! We can help kids cultivate basic coping techniques to overcome anxiety as well as life skills to find meaning, purpose, and engagement in their lives.

While I can't go back in time to help little Renee, I founded GoZen! in order to help a new generation of kids, parents and therapists. Peace is within reach—it comes from strength that lies within all of our children.

You can always reach me at *renee@gozen.com*. I'd love to hear from you!

Don't forget to grab your bonuses!
www.gozen.com/gotapping

Made in the USA
San Bernardino, CA
10 January 2017